BUCKINGHAM PALACE

I hope this souvenir programme will serve as a lasting memento of the Diamond Jubilee Weekend. I am delighted to send my good wishes to all those who will be involved in the special events, whether as volunteers, participants or spectators.

This memorable year will serve to remind us of the importance of family and friendship, examples of which my family and I have been fortunate to see in many forms during our Jubilee travels throughout the United Kingdom and the wider Commonwealth. It will also be a time to give thanks for the many achievements of the last six decades and to look to the future as we join together in our celebrations.

I send my sincere good wishes to you all.

Elizabeth R

His Royal Highness The Prince of Wales.
Photograph by Hugo Burnand ©HRH The Prince of Wales.

CLARENCE HOUSE

Ten years ago, I wrote that Golden Jubilees have happened only rarely in our history. A decade on, in 2012, I can say with confidence that a Diamond Jubilee is something even more remarkable. Both help us to celebrate a number of critical aspects of the life of this country and the Commonwealth, which can perhaps best be summarized as our common identity, the timeless threads of the traditions and history which bind us together and the continuity of our institutions. Over the last 60 years, The Queen has made an extraordinary contribution through her public service and, in doing so, has touched the lives of countless people around the world. Her Majesty's life and work have given a powerful expression to those cherished qualities of selflessness and duty which, in so many ways, have helped to transcend the immense changes in the last six decades.

This year's Diamond Jubilee celebrations have captured the imagination of a range of charitable community projects involving the Arts, the natural environment and volunteering initiatives. I can only hope these will help to develop further the essence of our individual and collective contributions to society – contributions which seek no financial reward or recognition, but which deliver outcomes to the enhancement of the public good… values and approaches which The Queen has encouraged ceaselessly for over half a century.

Whatever you are doing to help mark Her Majesty's Diamond Jubilee, I did just want to send you my heartfelt good wishes.

Three generations of the Royal Family before a dinner in 2003 to mark the 50th anniversary of Her Majesty's Coronation.

CONTENTS

The Queen, Prince Philip and their children in 2007.

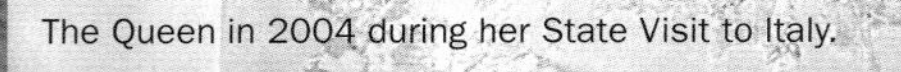
The Queen in 2004 during her State Visit to Italy.

The Queen and Princess Margaret in 1933.

The Royal Family in the grounds of Frogmore House, Windsor in 1968.

Prince William steals the show after the christening of Prince Harry in 1984.

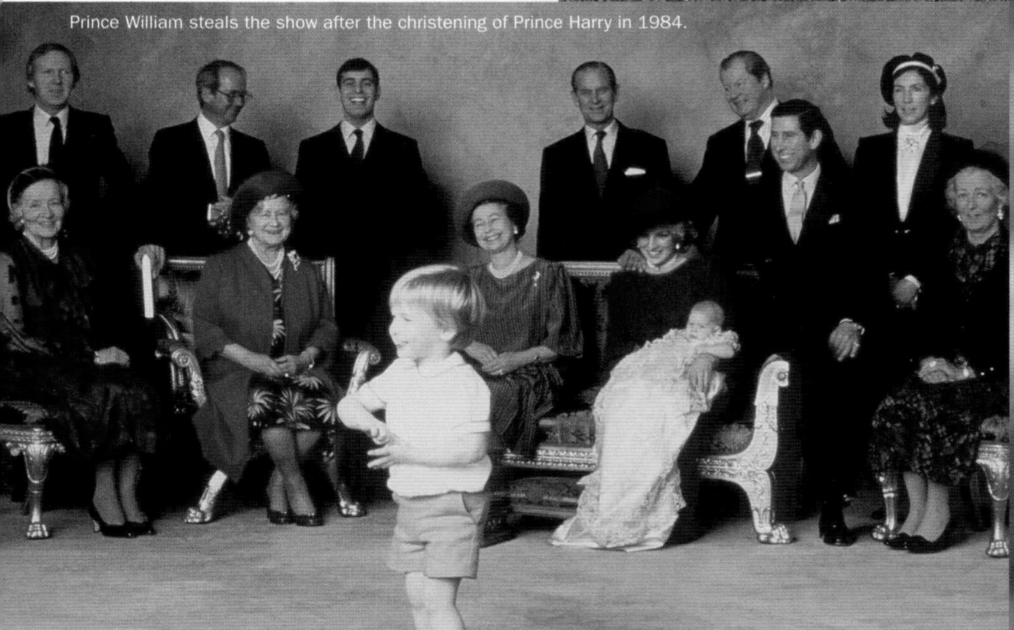

Trooping the Colour in 2005.

INTRODUCTION

The Queen's Diamond Jubilee, marking 60 years of her reign, is a special and rare celebration

It is a once in a lifetime opportunity to celebrate 60 years of service to the United Kingdom and the Commonwealth. In the hundreds of years of the British Monarchy, only one other Diamond Jubilee has been celebrated, that of Queen Victoria in 1897.

The celebrations culminate in four days of highly visual pomp, pageantry and festivities in June 2012, a national celebration which is also global, signifying 60 memorable years. In this, Her Majesty The Queen's Diamond Jubilee year, communities all over the United Kingdom and the Commonwealth are expressing their thanks for six decades of dedicated service.

This publication celebrates the exceptional milestone of a Diamond Jubilee. The first chapter outlines the events of the Diamond Jubilee central weekend, 2nd-5th June, which are the focal point of the Jubilee festivities, with the Big Jubilee Lunch, Thames Pageant, Diamond Jubilee Concert and Beacons as well as a Service of Thanksgiving at St Paul's Cathedral.

The second chapter, "Jubilation", contains information about some of the exciting Diamond Jubilee celebrations in 2012, in the United Kingdom and internationally.

The third chapter tells the story of the momentous 60 years of The Queen's reign, which has seen not only landmark events in Her Majesty's life, but also enormous social, technological and other changes.

The fourth chapter documents previous Royal Jubilee celebrations, including the festivities for The Queen's Silver Jubilee in 1977 and Golden Jubilee in 2002.

Over the years, The Queen has adapted the institution she so nobly heads to the pace of change. At the same time she has made a profound impact on the United Kingdom.

That she rose to the challenge, ably supported by The Duke of Edinburgh and the other members of the Royal Family, is a remarkable achievement.

The Official Souvenir Programme has been designed & published by
Publications UK Ltd
Tel: +44 (0)20 8238 5000
Fax: +44 (0)20 8238 5001
Email: info@publicationsuk.co.uk
Web: www.publicationsuk.co.uk

We are grateful to the Royal Household for their help and cooperation in producing this publication.

Managing Director: Stewart Lee
Editor: Thomas Corby MVO
Art Direction & Design: Hitesh Chauhan
Research & Production: Roshan Adam
Advertising: Ruth Levine

Picture Credits: The Bridgeman Art Library; Nadia Huggins, Camera Press (Marcus Adams, Bassano, Cecil Beaton, Anthony Buckley, Hugo Burnand, Illustrated London News, David Secombe, John Swannell); Getty Images; The Press Association; The Royal Collection.

Distributed by Seymour Distribution Ltd.
Printed in the United Kingdom by BGP Goodhead.

Front cover Official Diamond Jubilee photograph of The Queen and The Duke of Edinburgh taken in the Centre Room in Buckingham Palace in December 2011. © Royal Household/John Swannell.

Back cover Official Diamond Jubilee photograph of The Queen taken in the Centre Room in Buckingham Palace in December 2011. © Royal Household/John Swannell.

Right Official portrait of The Queen on her 40th birthday in 1966. Photograph by Anthony Buckley, Camera Press London.

Crowds surge up The Mall for The Queen's Golden Jubilee celebrations, 4 June 2002.

CHAPTER ONE

THE DIAMOND WEEKEND

An Outline of the Main Events, 2nd - 5th June 2012

SATURDAY 2ND JUNE 2012

The Epsom Derby

The Queen will attend the Epsom Derby.

www.epsomderby.co.uk

SUNDAY 3RD JUNE 2012

The Big Jubilee Lunch

People come together to share lunch with neighbours, friends and family. This may take the form of a traditional street party or a picnic lunch in small or larger groups. The Duchess of Cornwall is the Patron of the Big Jubilee Lunch.

www.thebiglunch.com

The Thames Diamond Jubilee Pageant

A thousand boats from across the United Kingdom, the Commonwealth and around the world take part in a flotilla, with The Queen travelling in the Royal Barge. The Prince of Wales is the Patron of the Thames Diamond Jubilee Foundation.

www.thamesdiamondjubileepageant.org

MONDAY 4TH JUNE 2012

Diamond Jubilee Concert

A televised concert at the front of Buckingham Palace, organised by the BBC, featuring a line-up of musical stars from the worlds of rock and pop, along with the best of classical music and musical theatre.

www.bbc.co.uk/diamondjubilee

The Queen's Diamond Jubilee Beacons

A network of over 3,000 beacons are lit by communities and individuals throughout the United Kingdom, as well as the Channel Islands, the Isle of Man and the Commonwealth, with The Queen lighting the National Beacon.

www.diamondjubileebeacons.co.uk

TUESDAY 5TH JUNE 2012

Service of Thanksgiving and Carriage Procession

A Service of Thanksgiving at St Paul's Cathedral takes place, followed by a lunch at Westminster Hall, a Carriage Procession to Buckingham Palace and a Balcony appearance with a Flypast.

www.thediamondjubilee.org

THE EPSOM DERBY

Saturday 2nd June

The Queen's Diamond Jubilee celebrations will reach an exciting peak on the first weekend in June. They start with an occasion from which she invariably derives huge pleasure, the Derby on Epsom Downs, which she is attending on Saturday 2nd June.

In a fitting tribute to The Queen's long standing love of the turf, the Coronation Cup has been renamed the Diamond Jubilee Coronation Cup and has been moved from its traditional Friday slot to Derby Day.

In 1900, the winning horse in the Derby was called Diamond Jubilee, which had been bought by The Prince of Wales, as a tribute to his mother, Queen Victoria, for her landmark 60 year celebration in 1897.

Throughout her reign, Her Majesty has nurtured the ambition to emulate the sporting luck of so many of her Royal predecessors in the greatest race in the calendar of the turf. Despite ten runners in the Derby, the nearest she has come was with the brilliant Aureole, a tantalising second in 1953, the year of her Coronation.

The Queen has a deep affection for horses stretching back to her childhood. The racecourse is probably the one place where she can escape the pressures of official duties and she is often seen punching her fists in the air and cheering her favourite on like any other race goer.

Left The Queen's horse Carlton House (2nd right) in the 2011 Derby.

Clockwise from above Derby Day moments from 1993, 2011, 2011, 1991, 2002.

THE BIG JUBILEE LUNCH

Sunday 3rd June

The Big Jubilee Lunch takes place on Sunday 3rd June and encourages people to come together to share lunch with neighbours, friends and family. This could be a street party, or a gathering in a back garden, park or community hall. Research shows that holding Big Lunches has a lasting and deep impact on community relations.

The Duchess of Cornwall is the Patron of the Big Jubilee Lunch and the organisers have received a message of support from The Queen. More than 50 of the UK's largest community groups, membership organisations and charities are supporting the Big Jubilee Lunch, including the Scout Association, Rotary International in Great Britain and Ireland, Neighbourhood Watch and Age UK.

The Duchess of Cornwall is joined by children from St Peter's Primary School in Eaton Square on the day she took on the Patronage of The Big Jubilee Lunch, March 2012.

The Big Jubilee Lunch is run by the Eden Project, a United Kingdom social enterprise and charity. Since starting in 2009, thousands of Big Lunches have taken place in all kinds of communities, and in 2011 the number of participants doubled to the best part of two million. This year, a record number of people across the United Kingdom are expected to participate.

The Big Jubilee Lunch aims to reach large sections of the communities across every region of the United Kingdom. Of course there is a rich tradition in the United Kingdom of holding street parties to celebrate Royal landmark occasions, such as The Queen's Coronation in 1953, her previous Jubilees in 1977 and 2002, and last year's Royal Wedding of The Duke and Duchess of Cambridge.

Further information is available at:
www.thebiglunch.com

Actress Barbara Windsor with scouts promoting the Big Jubilee Lunch at Buckingham Palace in March 2012.

Typical Silver Jubilee street decorations.

A Big Lunch held in Wales in 2011.

MESSAGE

TIM SMIT KBE - CHIEF EXECUTIVE AND CO-FOUNDER, THE EDEN PROJECT.

We are delighted and honoured to be playing a part in the celebrations for Her Majesty The Queen's Diamond Jubilee.

On Sunday 3rd June, we hope that people across the length and breadth of the United Kingdom, around the Commonwealth and the rest of the world, across all time zones, communities will be getting together to celebrate our Queen's Diamond Jubilee by having a BIG JUBILEE LUNCH with their neighbours. Every event held will be unique and the product simply of the goodwill and imagination of the participants. In this special year, every event held will be unique to create a memory that will last a lifetime and, we sincerely hope, start a habit that will turn the first Sunday in June into our own British version of Thanksgiving.

As we all know, the British are hopelessly shy, quiet, unassuming, self-deprecating and keep themselves to themselves – except when there's a good excuse for a party! When thawed out the British are legendary and for the last three years, people across the United Kingdom, in small groups, in lighthouses, in streets, across hamlets, villages, towns and cities, have been deciding, in ever increasing numbers to celebrate their neighbourhoods with – their neighbours.

Big Lunches can be anything from a shared sandwich and a glass of pop, to a right Royal feast. Everyone taking part agrees that it is good to feel connected to something bigger, to belong to a community. Breaking bread and putting aside just a few hours once a year goes a long way to making us feel happy to be where we are. It isn't just the lunch – of course that's fun – it is the preparing for it that creates the glue that enables the day to become a cultural bond that inspiring thousands of other events and the creation of clubs of all descriptions that take place throughout the year.

That is why we called it THE BIG LUNCH and The Eden Project, where it all began, is proud to have lit the blue touch paper on a tradition that has informally existed for centuries and which, in an age of fragmented family groups and communities, feels more necessary than ever before.

THAMES
1952 DIAMOND JUBILEE 2012
PAGEANT

THE THAMES DIAMOND JUBILEE PAGEANT

Sunday 3rd June

On 3rd June The Queen and other members of the Royal Family, travelling in the Royal Barge, will play the central role in the flotilla in The Thames Diamond Jubilee Pageant. At high water up to a thousand boats, a reflection of the maritime heritage of the United Kingdom and the Commonwealth, will muster on the River Thames. It will be one of the largest flotillas assembled on the river in modern times and will feature a seven mile long procession. The

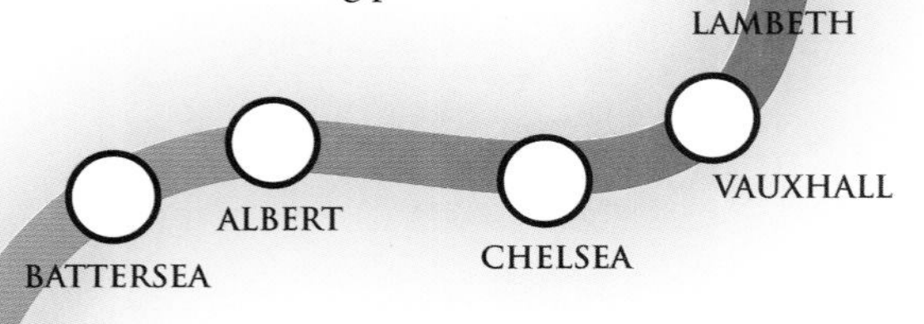

The Royal Barge. © Joseph Bennett.

WEST INDIA DOCKS

GREENWICH

Prince of Wales will play a key role on the day as Patron of the Pageant.

The Royal Barge is a modern vessel, The Spirit of Chartwell, decorated and adorned to head the Royal section of the flotilla. A floating belfry with eight new bells and commissioned by the 17th century city church of Saint James Garlickhythe will herald The Royal Barge with its peals echoed by river bank churches.

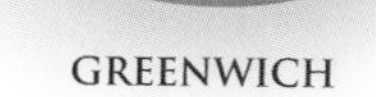

The flotilla will pass 14 bridges and take 75 minutes to pass any given point. The Royal Barge will stop at Tower Bridge for The Queen to review the flotilla as it passes.
Further information is available at:
www.thamesdiamondjubileepageant.org

MESSAGE

THE MARQUESS OF SALISBURY – CHAIRMAN, THAMES DIAMOND JUBILEE FOUNDATION.

One of the central events of the Diamond Jubilee celebrations will be the Thames River Pageant on Sunday 3rd June. A thousand boats, with The Queen in her Royal Barge, will process downriver. Her journey will be accompanied by the peal of bells, much music, the cheers of vast crowds and watched on large screens throughout the Kingdom. Also watching will be one of the biggest worldwide Television audiences in history. The river will have seen nothing like it since the days of Charles II, if ever.

It is an honour to be chairing the Thames Diamond Jubilee Foundation, organising this remarkable event to give our heart-felt thanks to The Queen for her sixty year reign.

I am also delighted that the river pageant will be a springboard for our charitable partners including The Queen Elizabeth Diamond Jubilee Trust.

We look forward with great excitement to cheering our Queen at what we hope will be the greatest show the Thames has ever seen.

THE DIAMOND JUBILEE CONCERT

Monday 4th June

On Monday 4th June Buckingham Palace will become the backdrop for the most ambitious single concert event ever staged by the BBC. A specially constructed, round stage designed by world-renowned architect Mark Fisher will encircle the historic Queen Victoria Memorial right in front of the Palace, onto which the biggest stars of music will be coming from across the globe to perform in front of Her Majesty The Queen and an invited live audience of thousands. Hundreds of thousands are expected to watch via screens along The Mall and in the adjoining Royal Parks, and millions more will be watching via television around the world.

Kylie Minogue.

Sir Tom Jones.

The Diamond Jubilee Concert will be a spectacular celebration of 60 years of The Queen's reign through music, and it will include the best of rock and pop performed by artists who have recorded in every decade of her reign. It will feature memorable and extraordinary collaborations between artists, including many from the Commonwealth, alongside gems from the worlds of musicals and classical music. The concert will make full use of the historic backdrop through stunning lighting, projections and pyrotechnics.

JLS.

Sir Paul McCartney. © 2011 MPL Communications Ltd / Photographer: MJ Kim.

Jessie J.

Sir Elton John. © Carl Studna.

Musical Director Gary Barlow has joined forces with the BBC to bring together an extraordinary line-up of performers for this once-in-a-lifetime event. Confirmed artists include: Shirley Bassey, classical tenor Alfie Boe, American soprano Renée Fleming, Jools Holland, Jessie J, JLS, Elton John, Grace Jones, Tom Jones, Chinese piano virtuoso Lang Lang, Annie Lennox, Madness, Paul McCartney, Kylie Minogue, Cliff Richard, Ed Sheeran, Robbie Williams and Stevie Wonder.

Ten thousand lucky ticket holders have been allocated seats for this unique event via a national ballot which took place in March. As well as the millions watching the concert on BBC One and BBC One HD, millions more will watch the concert the following day exclusively on ABC in America, and the event is expected to be broadcast in many more countries around the world. BBC Radio 2 will also be broadcasting the concert across the United Kingdom.

MESSAGE

GARY BARLOW – MUSICAL DIRECTOR, THE DIAMOND JUBILEE CONCERT.

Monday 4th June 2012 will mark an historic day in the British calendar. We're taking over the Queen Victoria Memorial in front of Buckingham Palace for what we hope will be one of the most memorable live music moments in UK history. We're pulling in the biggest music acts from the last six decades to perform for our Queen in what is set to be a very large crowd gathered in front of Buckingham Palace.

It is an honour to be involved in the Diamond Jubilee celebrations and to share in a fantastic musical celebration with our Queen and the great British public. I can't tell you how much I'm looking forward to being a part of this special day!

THE QUEEN'S DIAMOND JUBILEE BEACONS

Monday 4th June

Beacons will be lit around the world in honour of The Queen's Diamond Jubilee. More than 3,000 beacons will be lit by communities and individuals in a range of locations in the United Kingdom as well as Commonwealth Realms. The Queen will be lighting the National Beacon at around 10.30pm on Monday 4th June 2012.

Venues for beacon lighting include the Palace of Holyroodhouse and HM Tower of London, as well as the private Royal estates of Sandringham and Balmoral. There will also be beacons at Lambeth Palace and Bishopthorpe Palace, York.

Bruno Peek illuminates Clerkenwell Green, London in 1998.

Beacons are being taken to the top of the four highest Peaks in the United Kingdom by the following charities: Scafell Pike, England (Cancer Research UK); Ben Nevis, Scotland (Help for Heroes); Mount Snowdon, Wales (Walking with the Wounded); and Slieve Donard, Northern Ireland (Fields of Life). Sixty Beacons will also be lit along Hadrian's Wall. Significantly, a beacon will be lit at Treetops, in Kenya, where Her Majesty learnt that she had become Queen on 6th February 1952.

Beacon lighting spans hundreds of years, celebrating Royal Weddings, Jubilees and Coronations, illuminating village greens, castle battlements, church towers, farms, beaches, front gardens, mountain tops and even car parks. Beacon chains were once used for sending messages at times of national emergency, like the threat of the Spanish Armada, but have now become a symbol of unity across borders, countries, and continents. In 1897 beacons were lit nationally to celebrate Queen Victoria's Diamond Jubilee. In 1977 and 2002 beacons were lit to celebrate The Queen's Silver and Golden Jubilees.

Further information is available at:
www.diamondjubileebeacons.co.uk

MESSAGE

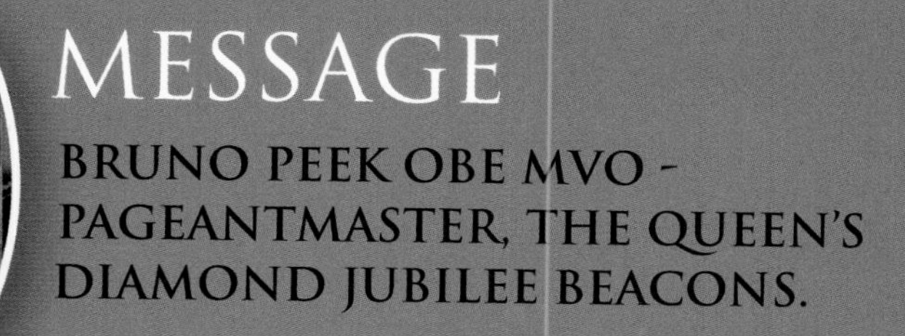

BRUNO PEEK OBE MVO – PAGEANTMASTER, THE QUEEN'S DIAMOND JUBILEE BEACONS.

In 2002 I had the honour of coordinating The Queen's Golden Jubilee Beacons. I will never forget the magical moment, when standing next to The Queen, I saw a rocket shoot down The Mall, to light the Queen's National Beacon located on the Queen Victoria Memorial. The reaction from the many thousands of people on The Mall that night was truly amazing.

For The Queen's Diamond Jubilee this year, I again have the honour of coordinating the lighting of over 3,000 Beacons throughout the United Kingdom, Channel Islands, Isle of Man, Commonwealth and the Overseas Realms and Territories to be lit on Monday 4th June 2012 in celebration of this most important moment in our history, and in The Queen's life too.

The reaction from the many communities, voluntary and charitable organisations, churches, local authorities, town and parish councils, cities, individuals, farmers and country estates that make up the fabric of our nation and Commonwealth has been astonishing.

This once-in-a-lifetime celebration will not only stay in the hearts and minds of those taking part but will also provide a lasting memory of a young woman who pledged herself to a lifetime of duty six decades ago.

Top The Queen lights a beacon floating in the Thames as she travels by boat to the Millennium Dome at Greenwich in 1999.

Middle The Queen lights the Trafalgar Weekend Beacon aboard HMS Victory in 2005.

Below A Golden Jubilee Beacon burns beside the Queen Victoria Memorial in 2002.

SERVICE OF THANKSGIVING AND CARRIAGE PROCESSION

Tuesday 5th June

Above The Queen and members of the Royal Family watch from the balcony as soldiers from the Welsh Guards fire a Feu de Joie (Fire of Joy), as part of The Queen's official 80th birthday celebrations in 2006.

Overview

The festivities on Tuesday 5th June will be the colourful climax of the four day national holiday weekend. Carriages, cascading gunfire, a huge armed services presence and military bands will provide scenes of glittering ceremony against the backdrops of Buckingham Palace and St Paul's Cathedral. At its heart will be an open carriage procession in which The Queen and The Duke of Edinburgh are joined by The Prince of Wales, The Duchess of Cornwall, The Duke and Duchess of Cambridge, and Prince Harry.

The celebrations will culminate in Her Majesty being joined by other members of the Royal Family on the Palace balcony for an RAF flypast, and a *Feu de Joie* – Fire of Joy - a cascade of rifle fire by The Queen's Guard, interspersed with bars of the National Anthem. The only time it has been performed in The Queen's presence before was for Her Majesty's 80th birthday.

Service of Thanksgiving

The Queen and members of the Royal Family will attend the National Service of Thanksgiving at St Paul's Cathedral, conducted by the Dean, the Very Reverend Dr David Ison. The Archbishop of Canterbury, the Most Reverend and Right Honourable Dr Rowan Williams, will preach and give the Blessing. Following a Litany of Prayer, the Bishop of London, the Right Reverend Richard Chartres will read the specially commissioned Jubilee Prayer which will also be used in churches nationwide and in Commonwealth countries.

The interior of St Paul's Cathedral.

The Cathedral Choir will be joined by the Choir of the Chapels Royal and the "Diamond Choir" comprising 40 children from all over the country to sing a specially composed anthem, "The Call of Wisdom." The anthem text has been drawn from the Book of Proverbs by Canon Michael Hampel, the Cathedral's Precentor, and set to music by the contemporary composer Will Todd. The State Trumpeters of the Household Cavalry, the Band of the Welsh Guards, and the Royal Air Force Fanfare Trumpeters will perform at the service. Personnel from all three services will line the Cathedral steps for Her Majesty's arrival and departure.

MESSAGE

THE VERY REVEREND DR DAVID ISON – DEAN, ST PAUL'S CATHEDRAL.

Throughout its history, St Paul's Cathedral has been the focus for national celebration and commemoration under God. Often referred to as the nation's church, it has been a place of prayer and pilgrimage for over fourteen hundred years and the scene of Royal Jubilees since 1897.

St Paul's is glad to be hosting the National Service of Thanksgiving for Her Majesty The Queen's Diamond Jubilee on Tuesday 5th June. The congregation will include a broad and diverse representation of the peoples of this nation and the Commonwealth and many more people will be able to share this great act of worship with us through the various broadcast media.

Together with its good news of the greatness of God's love for us, Christianity, as well as all the major faiths, calls us to be committed to love God and to serve our neighbours. The Queen epitomises this commitment in her life of prayerful devotion and enduring service. These qualities will lie at the heart of the service at St Paul's on this historic occasion.

There will be much to give thanks for this day and much strength to be drawn from the love of God and the affection of the people as Her Majesty continues her responsibilities as Queen and Head of the Commonwealth and her faithful dedication to the Church.

At St Paul's, we pray for her every day and will continue to do so in the years ahead.

Dr David Ison.

Receptions and Lunch

The Queen and The Duke of Edinburgh will then attend a reception at the Mansion House, and other members of the Royal Family will attend a reception at Guildhall. The Livery will afterwards host a Diamond Jubilee lunch in Westminster Hall attended by The Queen, Prince Philip, The Prince of Wales, The Duchess of Cornwall, The Duke and Duchess of Cambridge, and Prince Harry.

A Sovereign's Escort.

The Duke and Duchess of Cambridge on the Balcony of Buckingham Palace on their wedding day, alongside The Queen, The Prince of Wales and The Duchess of Cornwall, 29 April 2011.

Representatives of the sponsoring livery companies will be present, but the vast majority of the 700 guest list will comprise people from all over the country whose trade, craft or profession is represented by one of the many different liveries taking part, together with the charities, schools and other organisations they support. The National Children's Orchestra of Great Britain will perform a programme of music at the lunch.

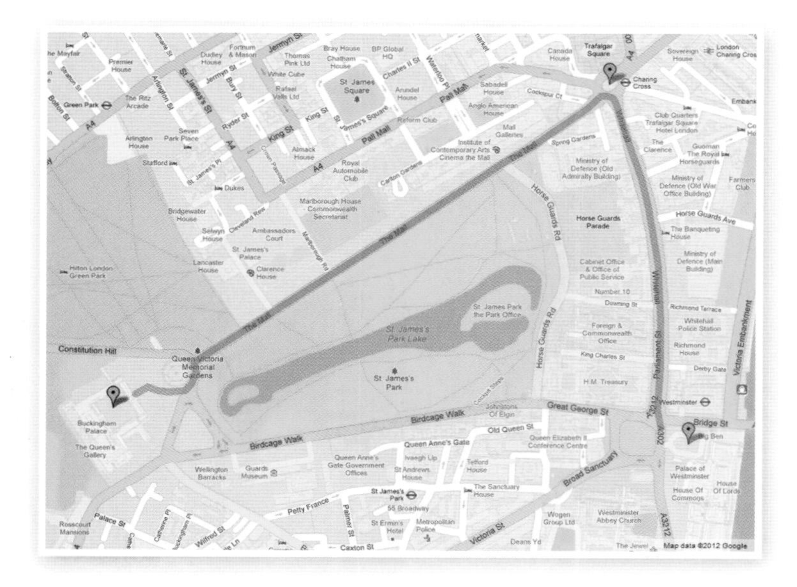

Above A map of the carriage procession route on 5 June 2012 from the Palace of Westminster to Buckingham Palace (via Trafalgar Square).

Procession and Balcony Appearance

Following the lunch the Royal party will travel along the processional route to Buckingham Palace. The Queen and The Duke of Edinburgh will use the maroon and gold leaf decorated 1902 State Landau, built for King Edward VII. The Duke and Duchess of Cambridge returned from Westminster Abbey in the Landau after their wedding in 2011. The Household Cavalry Mounted Regiment – The Life Guards and The Blues and Royals – will provide a Sovereign's Escort of nine Officers and 109 other ranks, and the Mounted Band of the Household Cavalry will ride ahead of the procession.

The route will be lined with more than 1,000 personnel from all three Services: from Royal Navy ships, submarines, the Fleet Air Arm, Naval land establishments and the Bands from the Royal Marines; from the Army's Grenadier, Coldstream, Scots, Irish and Welsh Guards of the Household Division, The Princess of Wales's Royal Regiment and the Household Division Bands; troops from The Royal Air Force's Queen's Colour Squadron, 63 Squadron RAF Regiment, and the Royal Air Force Band. The King's Troop Royal Horse Artillery will fire a 60 Gun Royal Salute from Horse Guards Parade to coincide with the carriage procession.

The Duke and Duchess of Cambridge drive in the State Landau after their 2011 wedding.

THE GUARDS ON PARADE

Tuesday 5th June

The troops of the Household Division are inextricably linked with the Sovereign and the Royal Family, and are invariably on parade for significant ceremonial occasions, such as The Queen's Birthday Parade – Trooping the Colour, the State Opening of Parliament and the visits of foreign Heads of State.

Uniquely Britain's ceremonial troops are all operational soldiers first and foremost. They will play a prominent role in the Diamond Jubilee celebrations of Her Majesty. The Queen is Colonel in Chief of the Armed Forces, The Duke of Edinburgh is Colonel Grenadier Guards, The Prince of Wales is Colonel of the Welsh Guards, The Duke of Cambridge is Colonel of the Irish Guards, The Princess Royal is Colonel of The Blues and Royals and The Duke of Kent is Colonel of the Scots Guards.

The Grenadier Guards

The Grenadiers are the most senior of the Foot Guards regiments, and their uniform collar is adorned with a "Grenade fired proper". Grenadier guardsmen wear a white plume on the left hand side of their bearskins. The regiment adopted the bearskin and was awarded the name 'Grenadier' by Royal Proclamation in 1815 after their defeat of the French Imperial Guard at Waterloo. The Regimental Motto - *Honi Soit Qui Mal Y Pense* – "Evil be to he who evil thinks" – is all about respect for others. Its ancient Royal origin reminds the regiment of its duty and loyalty to the Sovereign, and also the fundamental respect that underpins all it does.

The Coldstream Guards

Coldstream guardsmen have a red plume on their bearskins, worn on the right side. Their Regimental Motto, *Nulli Secundus* – "Second to none" – is the perfect summary of the excellence the regiment demands of itself in everything it does.

The Scots Guards

Scots guardsmens' bearskin caps have no plume. The Regiment's Motto, *Nemo Me Impune Lacessit* – "No one touches me with impunity" – encapsulates perfectly the war-fighting ethos and indomitable will to win that is the hallmark of the regiment's soldiering.

The Irish Guards

A blue, rather than an Irish green, plume was selected for the regiment's headgear because blue is the colour of the mantle and sash of the Knights of the Order of St Patrick, Ireland's highest order of chivalry, from which the regiment draws its cap star and motto. In addition, the uniform of the Royal Dublin Fusiliers, which was still in existence at the time the Irish Guards were formed, was a scarlet tunic and bearskin with a green plume. To prevent confusion, the Irish Guards opted for the blue plume of St Patrick. The Regimental Motto, *Quis Separabit* – "Who will separate us" – is derived from a Biblical quotation reminiscent of the regiment's wider ideals, and also reaches to the heart of loyalty.

The Welsh Guards

The regiment's motto, is *"Cymru am Byth"* – Wales Forever – an ancient battle cry which underlines loyalty to country, and its constituent nations. The regiment's white and green plume is set to the left of its bearskin cap.

THE HOUSEHOLD CAVALRY

The Life Guards

The Life Guards were originally raised in 1660. While in exile King Charles II commanded members of his personal body guard to form a new regiment. These men were loyal cavaliers who had smuggled the young King out of England after the execution of his father, King Charles I. The Life Guards are the senior regiment of the British Army, and their cap badge is the Royal cipher. The Regimental Motto, written in old French, is *"Honi Soit Qui Mal Y Pense"* – Shame upon he who thinks evil of it, – set in the Garter Star, Britain's oldest symbol of the chilvalry.

The Blues and Royals

In 1661, Charles II re-formed the Royal Regiment as his personal body guard and renamed it as the Royal Regiment of Horse. Thereafter, it became known as the Royal Horse Guards (The Blues). In the same year, The King also raised a third cavalry regiment, The Tangier Horse. It was subsequently renamed the Royal Dragoons (1st Dragoons). In 1969, the two Regiments merged to form The Blues and Royals. The Blues and Royals wear dark blue tunics instead of The Life Guards' red. They are also distinguished by different colour helmet plumes, numbers of buttons and insignia.

King's Troop Royal Horse Artillery

The King's Troop, Royal Horse Artillery is a ceremonial unit of the British Army. It is a mounted unit and all of its soldiers are trained to drive a team of six horses that pull each of the six First World War-era 13-pounder state saluting guns. Its duties include the firing of Royal Salutes in Hyde Park on both Royal Anniversaries and State Occasions, and providing a gun carriage and team of black horses for State and Military funerals. For the Diamond Jubilee the Troop will fire a gun salute on Horse Guards Parade at 1pm on 2nd June, and a 60 gun salute from the same location on 5th June throughout the duration of the Carriage Procession from the Palace of Westminster to Buckingham Palace.

Grenadier Guards
Single buttons white plume, left of cap.

Coldstream Guards
Buttons in pairs red plume, right of cap.

Scots Guards
Buttons in threes no cap plume.

Irish Guards
Buttons in fours blue plume, right of cap.

Welsh Guards
Buttons in fives white & green plume, left of cap.

Life Guards
Red tunic. White plume.

Blues and Royals
Dark blue tunic. Red plume.

The Queen and Prince Philip in the Pacific Islands, 1982.

Nigerian artist Chinwe Chukwuogo-Roys' portrait of The Queen painted to mark the Golden Jubilee in 2002.

The Queen in New Zealand, 1977.

The Queen in Australia, 2011.

The Queen in India, 1997.

The Queen and Prince Philip in Tuvalu, 1982.

COMMONWEALTH
SECRETARIAT

A MESSAGE

From His Excellency Kamalesh Sharma - The Commonwealth Secretary-General

We in the Commonwealth are fortunate to be headquartered in the heart of a Royal Park, at Marlborough House – part of St James's Palace. The Queen graciously granted us use of the house for the Commonwealth. We are deeply grateful for this exceptional and practical expression of Her Majesty's personal commitment to the Commonwealth.

We are also delighted that The Queen's Diamond Jubilee celebrations will have at their heart the relationship between Her Majesty and the Commonwealth. As Head of the Commonwealth, The Queen has been the symbol of our free association throughout the sixty years of her reign and is the keystone in our vast Commonwealth arch which spans the globe.

In her first Christmas broadcast in 1952, The Queen referred to the Commonwealth as "a most potent force for good, and one of the true unifying bonds in this torn world." These words remain equally true today, now that the Commonwealth encompasses a third of the world's population living in 54 member countries.

The Queen represents all that is best in the Commonwealth. Her lifetime of service continues to inspire rising

generations of Commonwealth citizens to build for a secure future based on mutual respect and understanding, where all states are accorded dignity regardless of endowment or stage of development, and in which there is equity and freedom of opportunity for all.

Through united and practical action to advance our shared values of democracy, development and diversity, the Commonwealth – with The Queen as Head – strives collectively for a future of promise for all Commonwealth citizens.

Kamalesh Sharma

Prince Harry in step with a group of dancers during his Caribbean tour, 6 March 2012.

CHAPTER TWO

JUBILATION: THE WORLD CELEBRATES

An Outline of United Kingdom and Worldwide Diamond Jubilee Visits and Events

The Queen's Diamond Jubilee will be celebrated around the world. Her Majesty and Prince Philip will be travelling widely across England, Scotland, Wales and Northern Ireland, while other members of the Royal Family will travel overseas, including to all Commonwealth Realms.

The United Kingdom regional tour covers all regions of the United Kingdom, starting in Leicester on 8th March, where The Queen and Prince Philip were accompanied by The Duchess of Cambridge, and finishing on the Isle of Wight and the New Forest on 25th July. The visits afford Her Majesty the opportunity to express her gratitude for 60 years of support and loyalty.

Members of the Royal Family are travelling overseas representing The Queen throughout the Diamond Jubilee year, visiting every Realm (where The Queen is Sovereign) as well as undertaking visits to Commonwealth countries, Crown Dependencies and British Overseas Territories.

Right The Earl and Countess of Wessex meet young performers during a visit to St Lucia School of Music on the second day of a tour of the West Indies on which Their Royal Highnesses represented The Queen, 22 February 2012. © Nadia Huggins.

The Earl and Countess of Wessex set the ball rolling in the West Indies

The first of the overseas visits representing The Queen was made by The Earl and Countess of Wessex and started in St Lucia on 21st February, where they took part in the Independence Day celebrations. Moving on to Barbados, they visited Parliament where they received a Joint Address by both Houses. Prince Edward read a message from The Queen in which Her Majesty said she had noted the level of development the country had achieved during its 45

OVERSEAS VISITS BY MEMBERS OF THE ROYAL FAMILY

Members of the Royal Family will travel overseas representing The Queen throughout the Diamond Jubilee year, visiting every Realm as well as undertaking visits to Commonwealth countries, Crown Dependencies and British Overseas Territories.

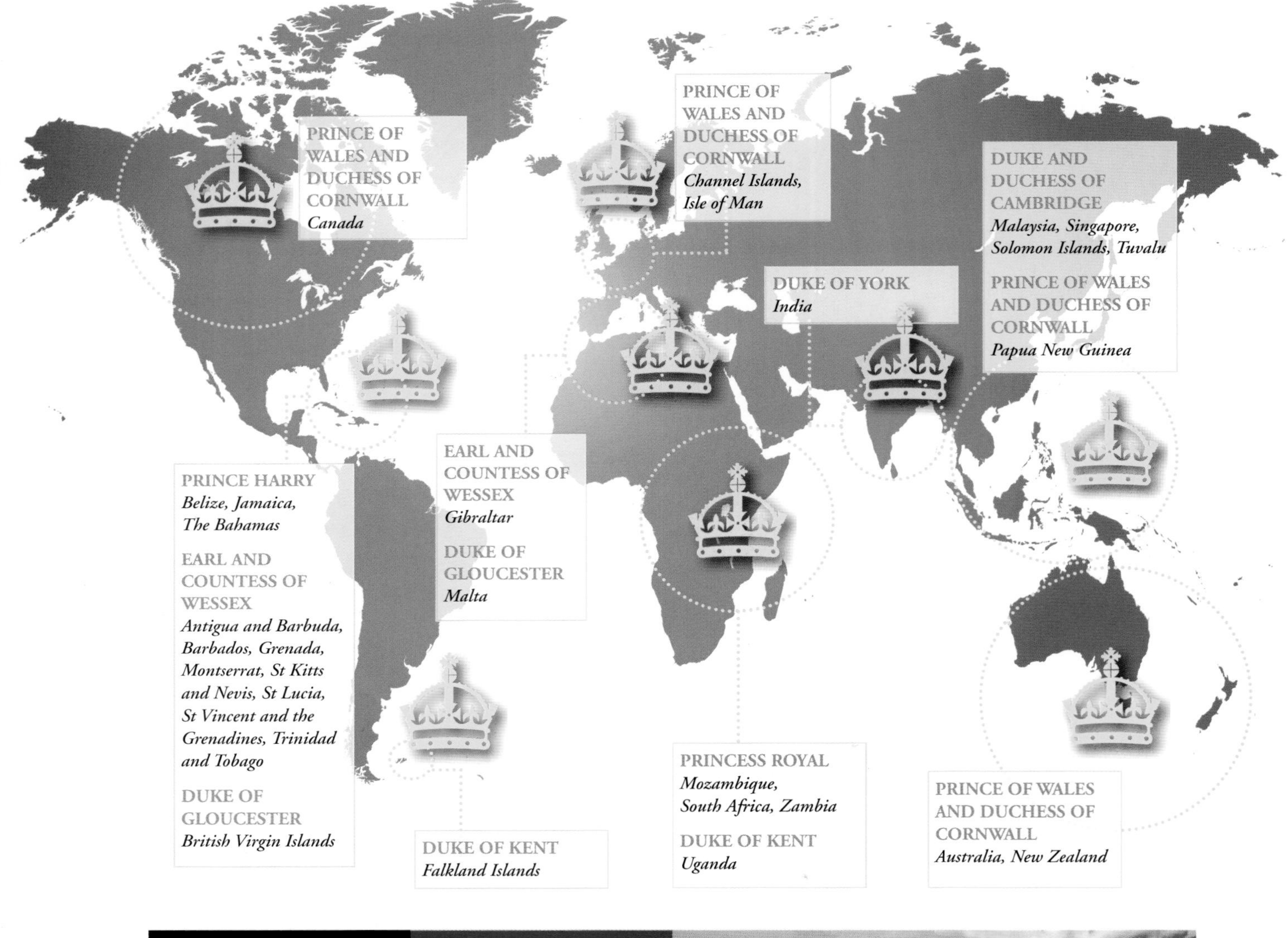

Prince Harry is first out of the blocks against Olympic sprint champion Usain Bolt at the University of the West Indies, Jamaica, 6 March 2012.

years of independence and called it a model small state for others around the world.

In Trinidad and Tobago, The Countess visited the Princess Elizabeth Centre, for children with special needs, which was built with funds given to The Queen, when Princess Elizabeth as a wedding present. In Montserrat, Their Royal Highnesses saw first hand the island's ongoing recovery from the devastating effects of the volcanic disruptions there. On their tour of the West Indies, Their Royal Highnesses also visited Antigua, Grenada, St Kitts and Nevis and St Vincent and the Grenadines.

Prince Harry follows on

Prince Harry's visit to the Caribbean in March was a great success. At a banquet in Kingston, Jamaica, he paid a heartfelt tribute to The Queen, praising her ability to combine her virtues as Head of State with her family role as a "wonderful, caring grandmother, to whom we, her grandchildren, are utterly devoted."

He said he counted it a great privilege to represent The Queen in Jamaica adding: "She is sad she can't be here, so you're stuck with me." Borrowing a lyric from a Bob Marley song he quipped: "But don't worry, coz every liddle ting gonna be aright." Earlier, Prince Harry won over Jamaican icon, Marley's widow, Rita. At a charity event in one of the poorest parts of Kingston he danced to the singer songwriter's "One Love," prompting Rita to remark: "Prince Harry's visit is a blessing." The music and dance performance at RISE Life which helps disadvantaged young people to develop their potential through music was attended by Gary Barlow, who was travelling around the Commonwealth recording local musicians for the song he is writing for the Diamond Jubilee.

Prince Harry meets Rita Marley, widow of singer Bob Marley, watched by Gary Barlow at a youth community centre in Kingston, Jamaica, 6 March 2012.

THE PROGRAMME OF UNITED KINGDOM REGIONAL VISITS AND ENGAGEMENTS

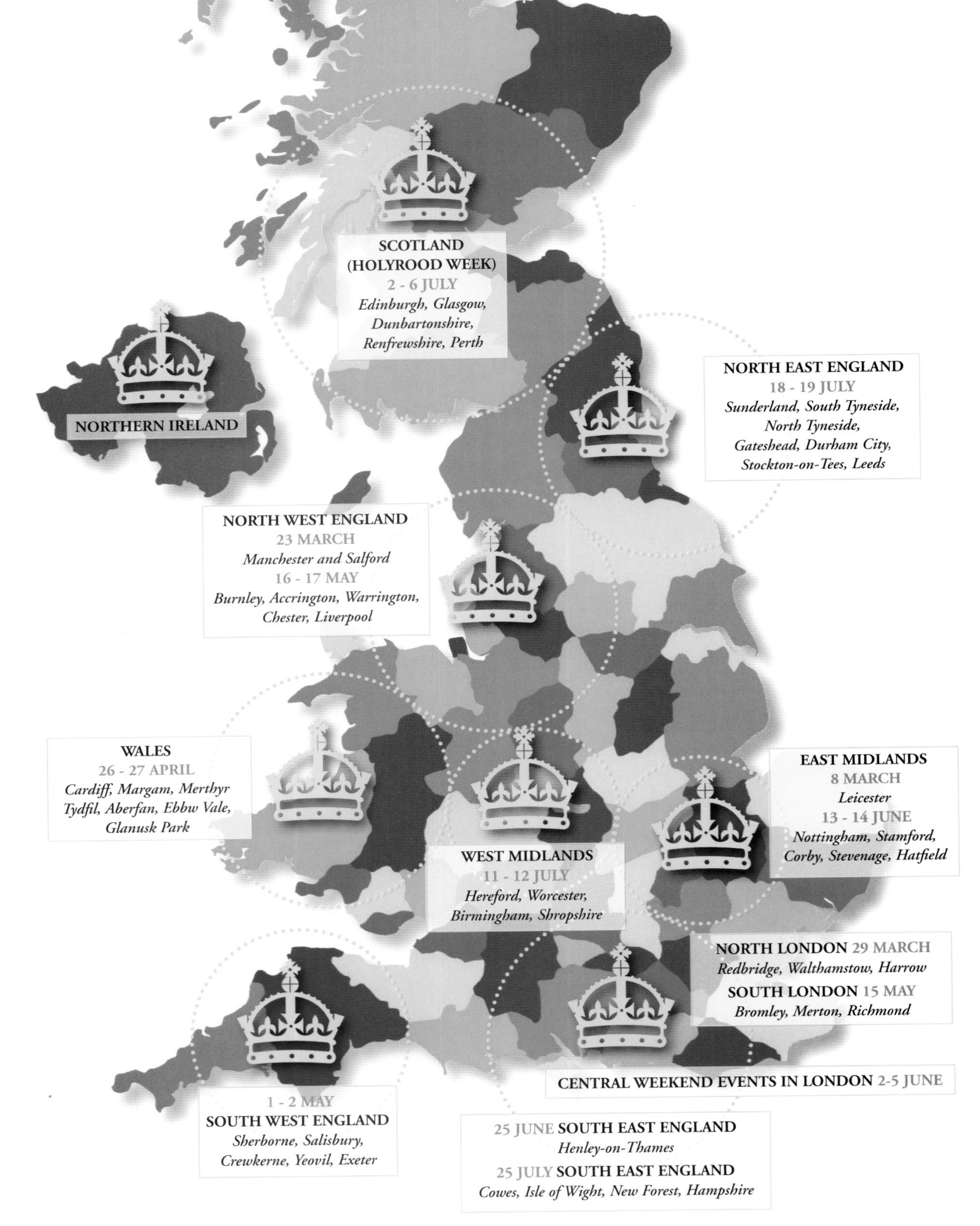

Right The Queen and The Duchess of Cambridge during the visit to Leicester, 8 March 2012.

The Prince also had an athletic encounter with Jamaican sprinter Usain Bolt, the fastest man on the planet, when with some ingenuity he out-paced the world record holder on a running track and thereafter dubbed him "the second fastest man in the world." Earlier on the first day of his Caribbean visit he named a road in Belmopan, the capital of Belize as The Queen Elizabeth II Boulevard, took part in a street party, visited an ancient historical site and laid a wreath at a memorial to British soldiers who had died whilst on active service in the Central American country.

UK Regional Tour begins in Leicester

The "away day" in Leicester on 8th March could have been described as an auger for the remainder of the United Kingdom tour. Tens of thousands of people turned out to greet The Queen, The Duke of Edinburgh and The Duchess of Cambridge. The Royal Party visited De Montfort University and watched a student fashion parade. Outside Leicester Cathedral, where Her Majesty attended a multi-faith service, an estimated 5,000 spectators burst into a spontaneous rendition of the National Anthem as The Queen emerged.

Queen Elizabeth Diamond Jubilee Trust

The Commonwealth is integral to the Diamond Jubilee celebrations and as part of these a new Trust has been launched to fund Commonwealth projects.

The Queen Elizabeth Diamond Jubilee Trust has been established to honour The Queen for a lifetime of service to the Commonwealth. The Trust will focus on enriching communities – both socially and culturally – making a real and lasting impact on the lives of those who live within the Commonwealth, across all generations and geographical boundaries.

The Queen leaving the Commonwealth Day Observance at Westminster Abbey, London, 12 March 2012.

The Trust will work with carefully selected partner charities and organisations with a successful track record to deliver iconic projects that are a fitting and enduring tribute to The Queen. Further information about the Trust is available at: **www.jubileetribute.org**

Commonwealth Day

On Commonwealth Day, on 12th March 2012, The Queen and The Duke of Edinburgh led members of the Royal Family and faith leaders at the annual Commonwealth Observance Service at Westminster Abbey.

Billed as Britain's largest annual multi-faith gathering, it celebrated the 2012 Commonwealth theme "Connecting Cultures." Those taking part included South African jazz musician and civil rights advocate, Hugh Masekela; Canadian singer-songwriter, Rufus Wainwright; award winning Nigerian writer, Chimamanda Ngozi Adichie and renowned primatologist and environmentalist, Dame Jane Goodall. The Scottish Poet, Liz Lochhead read a specially commissioned poem.

Jubilee Time Capsule

More than 1,000 children from schools and youth groups attended, every one of them having submitted an entry to the Royal Commonwealth Society's digital history project, the Jubilee Time Capsule, which is to be sealed later this year (the best entries will be presented to Her Majesty as a legacy of her Jubilee). The Jubilee Time Capsule has received more than 30,000 special stories and memories from 49 countries. Princess Eugenie has contributed, as have a range of well-known figures and personalities. The Dean of Westminster, The Very Reverend Doctor John Hall recalled welcoming Miss Catherine Middleton to the Abbey on her wedding day; paralympic athlete Oscar Pistorius remembered his childhood realisation that disability is not always a disadvantage, and a National Parks employee in Kenya shared his memories of the day that the then Princess Elizabeth found out about the death of her father King George VI.

Memories of The Queen and the Commonwealth are legion, and in the coming months will be revived as the celebrations in the overseas realms gain momentum. In the United Kingdom, as Her Majesty travels across its length and breadth, new memories and experiences will be etched in the national consciousness.

Diamond Jubilee Pageant

Another major event of the Jubilee is the Diamond Jubilee Pageant taking place on the evenings of 10th, 11th, 12th and13th May at Windsor Castle. Over 550 horses and more than 1,000 dancers, musicians, and performers from around the world are coming together each night in a performance to pay tribute to 60 years of The Queen's reign.

The Royal Collection in Diamond Jubilee Year

The Royal Collection has organised a programme of exhibitions at Buckingham Palace, Windsor Castle and the Palace of Holyroodhouse, as well as a touring exhibition to five UK venues to mark the Diamond Jubilee.

The Girls of Great Britain Tiara, 1893, R & S Garrard.
Royal Collection © 2012, Her Majesty Queen Elizabeth II.

The special exhibition at the Summer Opening of Buckingham Palace, "Diamonds: A Jubilee Celebration," shows the many ways in which diamonds have been used by British Monarchs over the last 200 years. The exhibition includes a display of a number of The Queen's personal jewels – those inherited by Her Majesty or acquired during her reign.

In addition, The Queen's Gallery, Buckingham Palace, presents the largest ever exhibition of Leonardo da Vinci's studies of the human body. Leonardo has long been recognised as one of the great artists of the Renaissance, but he was also a pioneer in the understanding of human anatomy. Today his drawings are among the Royal Collection's greatest treasures.

At Windsor Castle, "The Queen: Sixty Photographs for Sixty Years" includes the work of leading press photographers of the past six decades. The exhibition presents a portrait of The Queen's reign as captured in fleeting moments on both official occasions and at relaxed family gatherings.

At The Queen's Gallery, Palace of Holyroodhouse, over 100 of the finest works of art from the Royal Collection are on display. The exhibition "Treasures from The Queen's Palaces" has been selected from nine royal residences, across the entire breadth of the Royal Collection, and from over five centuries of Royal collecting. It includes paintings, drawings, miniatures, watercolours, manuscripts, furniture, sculpture, ceramics and jewellery.

The Williamson Brooch, 1953, Cartier.
Royal Collection © 2012, Her Majesty Queen Elizabeth II.

Diamond Jubilee Exhibitions

The Queen: 60 Photographs for 60 Years
The Drawings Gallery, Windsor Castle
4 February – 28 October 2012

Treasures from The Queen's Palaces
The Queen's Gallery, Palace of Holyroodhouse
16 March – 4 November 2012

Leonardo da Vinci: Anatomist
The Queen's Gallery, Buckingham Palace
4 May – 7 October 2012

Diamonds: A Jubilee Celebration
The Summer Opening of Buckingham Palace
30 June – 8 July and 31 July – 7 October 2012

Ten Drawings by Leonardo da Vinci: A Diamond Jubilee Celebration A Royal Collection Touring Exhibition
Birmingham Museum and Art Gallery
13 January – 25 March 2012

Bristol Museum & Art Gallery
30 March – 10 June 2012

Ulster Museum, Belfast
15 June – 27 August 2012

The McManus: Dundee's Art Gallery & Museum
31 August – 4 November 2012

Ferens Art Gallery, Hull
10 November 2012 – 20 January 2013

The Diamond Jubilee Emblem

The Diamond Jubilee Emblem was designed by 11-year-old Katherine Dewar from Chester. Katherine was chosen from 35,000 entries in a nationwide competition run by BBC children's programme Blue Peter.

Katherine Dewar displays her winning design, 29 March 2011.

The design, which has a crown poised above the Union Flag is flanked by columns of diamonds. The Blue Peter competition was open to children aged six to 14, and the top 30 children attended a special tea party at Buckingham Palace to celebrate their achievements.

The Queen views the work of the competition finalists at Buckingham Palace, 29 March 2011.

The Queen at the Krishna Avanti School in Harrow, as part of the Diamond Jubilee regional tour, 29 March 2012.

A MESSAGE

From The Rt. Hon. Sir John Major, KG, CH - Chairman, The Queen Elizabeth Diamond Jubilee Trust

As Her Majesty The Queen celebrates her Diamond Jubilee, she does so as the second longest serving Monarch in a thousand years of British history. Her Majesty is Head of a Commonwealth of two billion people, in 54 countries.

At the Commonwealth Heads of Government Meeting in Perth last October, it was unanimously agreed to establish The Queen Elizabeth Diamond Jubilee Trust, to honour Her Majesty's extraordinary lifetime of service. I am delighted and honoured to have been invited to Chair the Trust.

The Trust aims to raise funds from Governments, individuals, organisations and the corporate sector, to invest in projects that will make a real and lasting impact on the lives of people – of all generations – throughout the Commonwealth, in order to provide a lasting legacy for Her Majesty The Queen.

John Major

John Major

The Queen photographed by Cecil Beaton after her Coronation, 2 June 1953.

CHAPTER THREE

SIXTY DIAMOND YEARS

A Narration of Her Majesty's Life and Reign

A Consummate Monarch

The reign of The Queen has encompassed jet engine travel, space discovery, a multi-media culture, global terrorism, social revolution and world-wide political upheaval. Its landmarks have also been those of the history of the 20th century, and now the 21st.

She is the second longest reigning Sovereign in the history of the British Monarchy, ranking with George III who was King between 1760 and 1820; only her great-great grandmother, Queen Victoria, who occupied the throne for almost 64 years, has reigned longer. During her 60 years as Sovereign, she has emerged as the consummate master of her role, and her destiny – and following the death of Queen Elizabeth, The Queen Mother, as the matriarch of her family.

Throughout a reign in which public opinion has swung from adulation, in the early years, to satire, troughs of indifference, and now to deep and unreserved respect, she

The Queen returns to Buckingham Palace after Trooping the Colour in 1963.

US President Ronald Reagan with The Queen at Buckingham Palace in 1984.

US President Bill Clinton and The Queen at Buckingham Palace in 2000.

The Queen and US President Barack Obama at Buckingham Palace before the State Banquet in his honour in 2011.

US President John F. Kennedy and his wife Jacqueline with The Queen at Buckingham Palace in 1961.

South Africa's Nelson Mandela and The Queen process up The Mall on the first day of his State Visit in 1996.

The Queen presenting the Order of Merit to Mother Teresa in 1983.

France's Nicolas Sarkozy arrives for the State Banquet hosted by The Queen in his honour in 2008.

The Queen and Prince Philip with Indira Gandhi in New Delhi, 1983.

Pope John Paul II greets The Queen at the Vatican in October 2000.

Irish President Mary McAleese with The Queen in Dublin during Her Majesty's State Visit to the Irish Republic in 2011.

The Queen, accompanied by Prime Minister David Cameron, visits 10 Downing Street in June 2011 and views photographs of previous Prime Ministers.

has remained self-sufficient, proficient in the business of Monarchy, and comfortable in its familiar routines: the official visits at home and overseas, receiving ministers and ambassadors; the grand ceremonial occasions, like the visits of other Heads of State; reading, which she is quick at, and more importantly, understanding the State papers which follow her everywhere in their red boxes, even on holiday. She has attended every opening of Parliament since 1952 (except those in 1959 and 1963 when she was pregnant), giving the speech from the Throne, setting out her government's legislative programme.

The Queen at the State Opening of Parliament in 2004.

Other occasions punctuate her life: her annual Birthday Parade, known as Trooping the Colour; the service and ceremony of the Royal Order of the Garter, at Windsor Castle; the investitures, audiences with incoming foreign Ambassadors; the Royal garden parties, and the "Away Days" when she meets her people. She has welcomed 102 foreign Heads of State to Buckingham Palace, Windsor Castle and the Palace of Holyroodhouse on official State Visits.

During her reign Her Majesty has seen the old habits of deference and restraint vanish, but she has adroitly changed the institution she so nobly heads to subtly keep pace with change, and in doing so has preserved our unique brand of Monarchy for future generations.

She is probably the best politically informed woman in Britain. Twelve Prime Ministers, from Winston Churchill to David Cameron, have been received each week in audience when Parliament is in session, and so it could be said that her accumulation of political knowledge is greater than any one of them.

They are listened to carefully, questioned and sometimes challenged. The prime ministerial audience is, to use the description of one holder of the office, "no push over." The Queen and Prime Minister are entirely alone; their conversations remain totally confidential and wholly unreported.

The Queen arrives for a dinner at 10 Downing Street in 1955 to mark the end of the premiership of Sir Winston Churchill, her first Prime Minister.

The Queen with Prime Minister Tony Blair, at Buckingham Palace in 2005.

The Queen with five of her Prime Ministers at a dinner to mark the 40th anniversary of her reign in 1992.
Top left to right: Lord Callaghan, Lord Wilson, and Sir Edward Heath. Front row: Sir John Major and Lady Thatcher.

Prime Minister Gordon Brown with The Queen during a reception for leaders of the Group of 20 Countries (G20) in 2009.

Prime Minister Harold Macmillan with The Queen at Oxford University in 1960.

BY APPOINTMENT TO HER MAJESTY THE QUEEN
MANUFACTURERS OF CHOCOLATES. BENDICKS (MAYFAIR) LTD
WINCHESTER

BENDICKS®

IT'S A ROYAL AFFAIR

2012 marks the 50th anniversary of Bendicks holding Her Majesty The Queen's Royal Warrant. Every box of Bendicks mints is inscribed with the words 'By Appointment to Her Majesty The Queen.'

It all began on unassuming Church Street in Kensington where Mr Oscar Benson and Colonel Dickson began making chocolates in the tiny basement of their shop. By combining the first syllables of each of their names, the "Bendicks" brand was born, and very quickly it developed an enviable reputation for high-quality chocolates leading to the opening of another shop in the heart of London's exclusive Mayfair.

Perhaps the most significant part of the Bendicks story was the mint creation by Oscar Benson's sister-in-law in 1931. The Bittermint – an intense mint fondant covered in 95% dark chocolate and individually wrapped in foil – has been a staple of upmarket dinner parties for generations.

It's no surprise then that Bendicks has dedicated over 80 years to producing fine chocolates made with the finest quality ingredients. The craftsmanship that has been passed down through the years has ensured that Bendicks, today, is highly respected for its range of premium quality, After Dinner Mints.

Around the World

Much of The Queen's time has been taken up with travel. There are few countries she has not visited, including many of the globe's microscopic dots, and although she represents a country the imperial power of which has long gone, she is invariably greeted with curiosity, affection and instant recognition wherever she goes. Foreigners see her as something rare and desirable.

Her throne is by far the best known of a diminishing collection, and the stability it represents in a deeply uncertain world is the object of a wider envy than is sometimes realised at home. Understanding its virtue does not require an appreciation of the intricacies of constitutional Monarchy. It transcends politics, even nationality; to admirers the world over, she is not just The Queen of the United Kingdom, but THE Queen.

Scarcely a year goes by when The Queen does not visit a Commonwealth country. As the Head of the Commonwealth, and Sovereign of 16 of the 54 member countries, she fervently believes in this disparate grouping which encompasses a quarter of the earth. She sees it as a force for good. The Commonwealth leaders have widely different political persuasions, but they are united in one thing: that they can trust her impartial judgement.

The Queen and Prince Philip on the Great Wall of China on the third day of their State Visit in 1986.

Children in carnival costumes greet The Queen during a visit to Trinidad in 2009.

The family group in Buckingham Palace after the wedding of The Duke and Duchess of Cambridge in 2011.
Photograph by Hugo Burnand/Clarence House, Camera Press London.

The Royal Family join The Queen and Prince Philip at a dinner hosted by The Prince of Wales and The Duchess of Cornwall at Clarence House to mark the Royal couple's Diamond Wedding anniversary in 2007.

The Family

To The Queen, duty is paramount but so is her family. For instance, when Prince Charles was a baby, it is said she even asked Winston Churchill to change the time of the weekly Prime Ministerial audience so that she could bathe him. In this, her Diamond Jubilee year, tributes from her grandchildren have been frequent, demonstrating an intimate relationship with their "wonderful" grandmother, a source of advice and guidance in so many things affecting their lives.

In a recent television documentary, the affection between Princes William and Harry, Princesses Beatrice and Eugenie, and their "Granny" was palpable, but as Prince Harry remarked about an outcome of a family debate over Prince William's choice of uniform for his wedding: "My Grandmother was right – as she always is."

Above A wartime study of Queen Elizabeth, Princess Elizabeth (standing) and Princess Margaret in 1943.

The Queen and Prince Philip in 2007 at Broadlands where they spent the first part of their honeymoon.

The Early Years

Princess Elizabeth Alexandra Mary of York was born at 2.40am on 21st April 1926 at 17 Bruton Street, Mayfair, the town residence of her maternal grandparents, The Earl and Countess of Strathmore. At the time she was third in line of succession to the throne after Edward, The Prince of Wales, and his younger brother, The Duke of York, her dutiful and conscientious father. Who would have thought that ten years and seven months later, the hugely popular King Edward would relinquish his Crown and Empire for the love of American socialite and divorcee, Mrs Wallis Simpson, or that the Princess's father, who succeeded his brother as King George VI, would die when only 56.

Princess Elizabeth became Heiress Presumptive to the Crown of the United Kingdom on 10th December 1936, when her uncle King Edward VIII abdicated over his determination to marry Mrs Simpson.

Princess Elizabeth[1]s sheltered family life ended that abdication day, and things would never be the same. She was just ten years old and the realisation that some time in the future she would be Queen was absorbed gradually.

Having been secure in the cocoon of her parents' London home, 145 Piccadilly, she had known little or nothing of the fast-growing constitutional crisis which was to engulf her family. She was puzzled by the crowds outside the house, the comings and goings of important visitors, and was awestruck at the sight of an envelope addressed to "Her Majesty, The Queen." "That's Mummy now, isn't it," she is reported to have said.

Princess Elizabeth and her sister, Princess Margaret, had to accustom themselves to a regime of formality and the limelight surrounding their parents a limelight which soon shone on them. They were described in the newspapers as "The darlings of the Empire," and their faces decorated biscuit tins, chocolate boxes, and calendars across the world. Princess Elizabeth, however, had long been a cover girl, appearing on the front cover of Time magazine in April 1929, when she was three years old.

Princess Elizabeth, aged 12, with attendant corgi in 1938.
Photograph by Marcus Adams, Camera Press London.

The Coronation of King George VI in Westminster Abbey on 12 May 1937. Princess Elizabeth and Princess Margaret watch the Coronation of their parents from the Royal Box. Francis Owen Salisbury (1874-1962).

King George VI was crowned on 12th May 1937. It was the last enactment of pomp and circumstance before Europe was plunged into war. The Princesses played a photogenic role, dressed alike in full length white silk and cream lace dresses, trimmed with golden coloured bows and gold-edged purple velvet robes. Each wore a specially designed light weight coronet.

Princess Elizabeth's account of the day, pencil written in an exercise book, and tied round with pink ribbon, is preserved in the Royal Library at Windsor. Dedicated to "Mummy and Papa, in memory of their Coronation, from Lilibet (her family name) by herself," its ingenuous freshness has lost nothing for the passing of the years, and sets the scene in Westminster Abbey even more effectively than the prose of official historians. She wrote: "I thought it all very, very wonderful, and I expect the Abbey did too."

The King and Queen (later Queen Elizabeth, The Queen Mother) had less than three years to restore and revitalise the Monarchy's post-abdication image before World War II was declared, and with their two daughters they set out to combine majesty with an equally popular image of a happy, united family, something to which millions of other happy, united families could relate.

King George VI, Queen Elizabeth and their daughters in Buckingham Palace in their Coronation robes in 1937. Photograph by ILN, Camera Press London.

Princess in Wartime

The tide of war was inexorable. The Princesses were "evacuated" to Windsor Castle, which once again played its historical role as a fortress. They continued with their lessons, knitted socks for the troops, "Dug for Victory" as exhorted by the government propaganda poster, as well as producing and acting in their own Christmas pantomimes.

The strategy of sending them to Canada was discussed, but The King and Queen decided that the Royal Family should stay together as a symbolic unit. Queen Elizabeth's attitude was summed up in her famous wartime utterance: "The Princesses would never leave without me; I would never leave without The King, and The King will never leave."

And so, to use the wartime vernacular, Princess Elizabeth "stayed put." She pleaded with The King to be allowed to "do her bit," the World War II expression for joining up in the armed forces, and she enlisted in the Auxiliary Transport Service (the ATS) in February 1945. Commissioned as number 239873 Second Subaltern Elizabeth Alexandra Mary Windsor, she took a course in motor mechanics and driving.

A wartime Christmas pantomime at Windsor, 1941. Princess Elizabeth starred as Prince Charming with Princess Margaret as Cinderella.

The identification of the Royal Family with a nation at war reached its patriotic peak on VE (Victory in Europe) Day, 8th May 1945. Buckingham Palace became the magnet for the rejoicing over the German surrender and Princess Elizabeth, in uniform, appeared on the Palace balcony with her parents, Princess Margaret, and the wartime Prime Minister, Winston Churchill.

Fifty years later, The Queen recorded in a broadcast her excitement and exhilaration, and how The King allowed her and Princess Margaret to slip away from the Palace and mingle incognito with the cheering, singing and dancing throng. It was their Cinderella moment in reverse. "I think," she said, "it was one of the most memorable nights of my life…all of us just swept along on a tide of happiness and relief."

Above The Royal Family on the balcony at Buckingham Palace with Britain's wartime leader, Winston Churchill, on VE Day, 8 May 1945.

Left Princess Elizabeth at the wheel during her World War II military service in January 1945.

Princess Elizabeth aged twenty in 1946.

Princess Elizabeth relaxes in South Africa at the time of her 21st birthday in 1947.

Post-War Princess

In 1947 Princess Elizabeth accompanied her parents and Princess Margaret on a visit to South Africa, and made what is widely regarded as the most celebrated broadcast of her life. It was her 21st birthday. Sixty-five years on her words retain their resonance. From Cape Town, she said: "I declare before you all that my whole life, whether it be long or short, shall be devoted to your service and the service of our great imperial family to which we all belong, but I shall not have the strength to carry out this resolution alone unless you join in with me, as I now invite you to do. I know that your support will be unfailingly given. God help me to make good my vow…"

It was an almost nun-like promise and for someone so young a commitment of remarkable self-sacrifice. At the time of her Silver Jubilee in 1977, she reaffirmed that lifetime pledge of service, making clear that she had no intention of retiring and that abdication was unthinkable. Borrowing from Shakespeare's *Antony and Cleopatra* she told her people: "Although that vow was made in 'my salad days, when I was green in judgement,' I do not regret or retract one word of it." It has proved the animating spirit of her reign. She meant it in 1947, in 1977, at the time of her Golden Jubilee in 2002 and now, without the slightest evidence of wavering, in this, the year of her Diamond Jubilee.

Princess Elizabeth and Prince Philip announce their engagement, 10 July 1947.

Love and Marriage

VE night was an historic occasion, but Princess Elizabeth, like so many sweethearts and wives, was waiting for her man to come home from the war. Prince Philip of Greece and Denmark was second in command of the Royal Navy destroyer HMS Whelp which was present in Tokyo Bay for the final Japanese surrender on 2nd September 1945. In March 1941, serving on HMS Valiant, he took part in the Battle of Cape Matapan, off the Peleponnese, against the Italian fleet and was mentioned in dispatches.

The descendant of a web of British, Greek, Danish, German and Russian royalty and a great-great grandchild of Queen Victoria, he had for years, because of the volatile nature of Greek politics, lived a nomadic life. He and Princess Elizabeth were distant cousins, and the friendship between them, which began on the eve of the war, blossomed over the years into a genuine, old fashioned romance.

Their engagement was announced in July 1947 and their wedding at Westminster Abbey, on 20th November 1947, was a welcome gleam of colour in the bleak post-war world of rationing and shortages.

Prince Philip had earlier become a naturalised British citizen, renouncing his Greek royal title, becoming plain Lieutenant Philip Mountbatten RN, but on the eve of

Top Princess Elizabeth and Prince Philip photographed at Buckingham Palace on their wedding day, 20 November 1947. Front, left to right includes: Queen Mary, Princess Andrew of Greece, Prince William of Gloucester, Prince Michael of Kent, The King and Queen, and Prince Philip's grandmother Princess Victoria, Dowager Marchioness of Milford Haven. Photograph by Bassano, Camera Press London.

Above The Queen views her wedding dress displayed in an exhibition at Buckingham Palace in 2007.

his wedding he was created Duke of Edinburgh, Earl of Merioneth and Baron Greenwich. Ten years later The Queen accorded him the style and title of a Prince of the United Kingdom. He has become Britain's longest serving consort and the oldest spouse of a reigning British Monarch.

After their honeymoon, Princess Elizabeth resumed her official duties and her husband his Royal Navy career. He was posted to Malta and for almost two years The Princess divided her time between the George Cross Island and Britain.

There were, however, clouds on the horizon. King George VI was seriously ill and Princess Elizabeth had to deputise for him on a number of official occasions. Accompanied by Prince Philip she took on the Commonwealth tour her parents had planned to make in early 1952.

Accession and Coronation

Princess Elizabeth became Queen while filming a rhinoceros in Kenya from the observation post known as Treetops in a giant fig tree, overlooking a waterhole in the Aberdare Forest game reserve, 3,000 miles from Sandringham House where her much loved father died in his sleep on 6th February 1952. It was sunrise in Kenya and an eagle was hovering over her head. Two water buck were fighting, and one was fatally wounded.

The Queen returns to the Treetops site in 1983.

The Queen leaves Buckingham Palace in the Gold State Coach for her Coronation on 2 June 1953.

Below Her Majesty arrives at Westminster Abbey on 2 June 1953.

There is a Kikuyu tribal legend that when two water buck meet in combat and one dies, this signals the death of a great tribal chief. As one observer wrote at the time, "A young girl climbed into a tree as a Princess and climbed down as a Queen." Two years later the tree house was burnt down by Mau Mau fighters waging a war against British rule. The Queen returned to the site in 1983 during a visit to Kenya and planted a new fig tree on the spot.

Following the news of her father's death, she immediately returned to London and was proclaimed Queen on 8th February, the 38th Monarch in line of descent from Egbert, King of Wessex from 802 to 839 and of England from 827 to 839; the 40th Monarch since William I, the Conqueror, who obtained the Crown of England by conquest in 1066, and the sixth Queen Regnant since Mary Tudor.

The Coronation of The Queen, Westminster Abbey, 2 June 1953. Prince Charles watches from the Royal Box standing between The Queen Mother and Princess Margaret. Terence Tenison Cuneo (1907-1996).

The Coronation was planned for 2nd June 1953. Queen Elizabeth II rode in the Gold State Coach through a canyon of roaring affection. The Mall was spanned with gold and azure arches, from which glittering crowns were suspended. More than 30,000 people camped out on the pavements around the Palace on the rain soaked Coronation eve, bedding down with blankets, eiderdowns, waterproofs, stools, spirit stoves, gramophones, radios, tinned food, tarpaulins, and even rubber dinghies. There were thousands more in The Mall. Tented camps were pitched in the Royal Parks to house the 60,000 troops marching in the procession and lining the route. It was a masterpiece of organisation.

Sixty years on the crowds will be out again to applaud her Diamond Jubilee procession. Once again there will be carriages, bands, fanfares and guardsmen on parade. The difference, symbolising six decades of social change, will be the entertainments designed for popular appeal, like the concert in which top class musicians will perform, overlooked benignly by Queen Victoria perched on her memorial – and particularly the presence of a whole new generation of younger members of the Royal Family, representing the future of our Monarchy.

The Queen, after the act of Crowning on 2 June 1953.

The Queen waves to the cheering crowds during her 2002 Golden Jubilee procession.

CHAPTER FOUR

ROYAL JUBILEES: A HISTORY

Royal Jubilees are rare occasions, marking landmark periods of time on the throne. Few British Monarchs have achieved reigns of 50 years, let alone 60

Queen Victoria in 1897.

Queen Victoria's Golden and Diamond Jubilees

The Golden Jubilee of Queen Victoria was celebrated on 20th and 21st June 1887 (her grandfather George III had reached his Golden Jubilee in 1809, becoming the first Sovereign to celebrate 50 years in a ceremonial style). On 20th June, Queen Victoria's day began quietly with breakfast under the trees at Frogmore, the resting place of The Queen's beloved Consort, Prince Albert. She then travelled by train from Windsor to Paddington and across the Royal Parks to Buckingham Palace for an evening banquet.

Fifty foreign Kings and Princes – Victoria was not called "The Grandmother of Europe" for nothing – together with the governing heads of Britain's overseas Colonies and Dominions attended. On the following day the little Queen rode in a gilded open Landau, drawn by six cream coloured horses to Westminster Abbey, escorted by Indian cavalry. She was the first Empress of India. She

Queen Victoria with her family at the time of her Golden Jubilee in 1887. She was known as "The Grandmother of Europe." Among those present were The Prince and Princess of Wales, later King Edward VII and Queen Alexandra; Prince George of Wales, later King George V; The Crown Prince and Princess of Germany; Prince William of Prussia, later the Kaiser, and Princess Alix of Hesse, the last Tsarina of Russia.
Laurits Regner Tuxen (1853-1927). Supplied by Royal Collection Trust/© Her Majesty Queen Elizabeth II 2012.

Queen Victoria arrives at St Paul's Cathedral for her Diamond Jubilee Service in June 1897.

could not be persuaded to wear a crown or a coronet, opting for a bonnet. Opposite sat her daughter, The Crown Princess of Prussia and The Princess of Wales.

The escort included her three sons, five sons-in-law, and nine grandsons and grandsons-in-law. On her return to the Palace she appeared on the balcony, where she was cheered by huge crowds. There was an evening banquet and a firework display.

Edith Sitwell, in her biography of Queen Victoria, *Victoria of England*, wrote of that day: "The matriarch, the grandmother of the future Emperor of Germany and of the future Empress of Russia, felt the shadow of her greatness spreading over the earth..."

Ten years later, Queen Victoria's Diamond Jubilee was marked by many celebrations, including a carriage procession to St Paul's, where a short service of thanksgiving was held in front of the Cathedral as The Queen was too lame to manage the steps. Seventeen carriages carried members of her family and Royal families from around the world, envoys and ambassadors. She was showered with gifts from all parts of the Empire, among them a bicycle from the Mayor of Coventry, which was graciously accepted.

She wrote in her journal: "A never to be forgotten day. No one ever, I believe, has met with such an ovation as was given to me, passing through those six miles of streets...The crowds were quite indescribable and their enthusiasm truly marvellous and deeply touching. The cheering was quite deafening and every face seemed to be filled with real joy. I was much moved and gratified."

King George V's Silver Jubilee

The Silver Jubilee of King George V and Queen Mary, was another Royal landmark. On 6th May 1935 The King and Queen drove to St Paul's for the traditional service of thanksgiving, and in the procession were his two granddaughters, Princess Elizabeth and Princess Margaret, in matching pink coats and hats.

Everywhere The King and Queen went there were huge crowds and The King was astonished by the warmth of his reception. "I am beginning to think they must really like me for myself," he said.

Every night of Jubilee week The King and Queen appeared on the Buckingham Palace balcony. There were official receptions, loyal addresses and street parties, and across the country flags and bunting decorated hundreds of public and private buildings.

The King's official biographer, Harold Nicolson, wrote of the people's deep affection for the Sovereign, as a symbol of patriotism, and the pride that Britain's Monarchy, unlike so many others, had survived. He said: "There was comfort in the realisation that here was a strong benevolent patriarch personifying the highest standards... There was gratitude to a man who by his probity had earned the esteem of the whole world."

But sadly The King had only seven months to live and his death set in chain the dynastic crisis which eventually brought his granddaughter to the throne as Queen Elizabeth II.

SATURDAY

THE ILLUSTRATED LONDON NEWS

SILVER JUBILEE NUMBER

The Latest Natural-Colour Photograph of the King and Queen.
A Silver Jubilee Portrait-Study of Their Majesties.

The first natural-colour photograph of their Majesties—taken in 1914—is published on the next page of this number.

Below The scene at St Paul's Cathedral when King George V and Queen Mary arrived with the Royal Family for The King's Silver Jubilee Service in May 1935. Princess Elizabeth and Princess Margaret can be seen left standing behind Edward, Prince of Wales. This picture, by Sir Frank Salisbury, hangs in London's Guildhall.

The Queen goes walkabout in the City of London during her Silver Jubilee in 1977.

The Queen's Silver and Golden Jubilees

In the summer of 1977 Britain erupted into a riot of red, white and blue. The Queen's Silver Jubilee, marking 25 years of her reign evolved as a runaway success and the principal participant said she was "floored" by the spontaneous explosion of excitement and displays of affection.

The newspapers were filled with depressing economic news, but somehow the notion of thanking the Monarch for 25 years of exemplary service appealed to the British sense of fair play. Union flags started to appear across the land, and by the time The Queen took her place alongside Prince Philip in the Gold State Coach to drive to St Paul's in June, the cheers could be heard across the nation.

The Prince of Wales, in uniform as Colonel of the Welsh Guards, followed on horseback, just as an earlier Prince of Wales, later Edward VII, escorted Queen Victoria on her Golden Jubilee. More than a million people packed The Mall. The evening before the Thanksgiving Service she lit one small flame at Windsor and a chain of bonfires spread throughout Britain and on across the world to Australia and New Zealand. In 1977 The Queen's walkabout through the streets of London resembled a re-coronation by popular acclaim. A public holiday and sunshine guaranteed the success of thousands of street parties all over the United Kingdom, and even radical councils were swept along on the patriotic tide. But as far as The Queen was concerned, the celebrations gave focus to her reign, and the life she had dedicated to service and duty.

The regional tours lasted into August. Her Majesty travelled more than 7,000 miles in Britain, and 50,000 miles during a tour of 12 Commonwealth countries. She was determined to be seen by as many people as possible. Her Private Secretary, Sir Martin (later Lord) Charteris described the mood of the nation: "The Queen," he said, "quite simply had a love affair with the country."

At the time of Her Majesty's Golden Jubilee in 2002 she summed up what she felt about the people of Britain and the Commonwealth. It was "gratitude, respect and pride." During the celebrations huge crowds, nationwide and overseas, returned the compliment. They wanted to show that they cared about this unpretentious lady, who at just over 5ft tall does not dominate physically, but whose presence and aura commands attention wherever she goes.

The Golden Jubilee year did not start well. Princess Margaret died on 9th February, and another poignant loss was the death seven weeks later of Queen Elizabeth, The Queen Mother, at the age of 101. But as the months went by the Jubilee gained momentum. The Queen and Prince Philip circumnavigated the globe, starting with visits to Jamaica, New Zealand and Australia.

It was the sixth time in her reign that she had travelled round the world on a single tour. She visited 70 cities and towns in England, Scotland, Wales and Northern Ireland over 38 days from May to August. People all over the world held street parties, garden parties and other events to celebrate Her Majesty's 50 year reign. Perhaps the "coolest" party was in the Antarctic, where 20 scientists of the British Antarctic Survey staged a celebration at a temperature of minus 20, including an outdoor feast, a ration of champagne, cricket on the sea ice, skiing and sledging.

A chain of 2,006 beacons was lit across the world; the length and breadth of the United Kingdom, the Channel Islands and the Commonwealth. There were fireworks and illuminations at Buckingham Palace and a pop concert, opened by Queen guitarist, Brian May, playing "God Save the Queen," from the Palace roof. At the end of the concert Prince Charles paid tribute to his mother, saying: "We feel proud of you, proud and grateful for everything you have done for your country and the Commonwealth over 50 extraordinary years, supported unfailingly throughout by my father." At the Service of Thanksgiving at St Paul's, the Archbishop of Canterbury, Dr George Carey, praised both The Queen and the Monarchy and quoted a line from Elizabeth I's Golden Speech, given in 1601, in which she told her Parliament: "Though God hath raised me high I count the glory of my crown that I have reigned with your loves." He told Elizabeth II that she too reigned "with our loves," adding that unlike so much in the modern world, the relationship between Sovereign and people had grown stronger and deeper with the passage of time.

Later The Queen spoke of "a pretty remarkable 50 years by any standards," adding: "There have been ups and downs, but anyone who can remember what things were like after those six long years of war, will appreciate what immense changes have been achieved since then. Not everyone has been able to benefit from the growth of wealth and prosperity, but it has not been for the lack of political will. I think we can look back with measured pride on the history of the last 50 years."

Prince William applauds as The Prince of Wales makes a speech in praise of his mother, on stage in the gardens of Buckingham Palace, after the second concert to commemorate her Golden Jubilee in June 2002.

THE ROYAL PARKS

Everyone at The Royal Parks would like to offer The Queen our congratulations on celebrating her Diamond Jubilee, a truly momentous occasion.

We are extremely proud of our unique history of hosting royal celebrations and are privileged to welcome The Queen back to the parks on this remarkable occasion.

From childhood weekends at Richmond Park's White Lodge to Trooping the Colour on Horse Guards Parade in St James's Park, London's eight Royal Parks continue to feature in The Queen's personal and public life.

We look forward to hosting more royal occasions and welcoming The Queen and her family back to the parks for many more years to come.

Linda Lennon CBE, Chief Executive,
The Royal Parks

60 FACTS ABOUT THE QUEEN

The Queen has reached many milestones during her 60 years - here are some facts you may not know

1 ***The Queen is the second longest serving Monarch. Only five other kings and queens in British history have reigned for 50 years or more. They are:***

- *Victoria (63 years)*
- *George III (59 years)*
- *Henry III (56 years)*
- *Edward III (50 years)*
- *James VI of Scotland and 1st of England (58 years)*

2 ***The Queen is the 40th Monarch since William the Conqueror obtained the Crown of England.***

3 ***Since 1952 The Queen has given Royal Assent to more than 3,500 Acts of Parliament.***

4 ***Over the reign, Her Majesty has given regular audiences to 12 Prime Ministers. They are:***

- *Winston Churchill 1951-55*
- *Sir Anthony Eden 1955-57*
- *Harold Macmillan 1957-63*
- *Sir Alec Douglas-Home 1963-64*
- *Harold Wilson 1964-70 and 1974-76*
- *Edward Heath 1970-74*
- *James Callaghan 1976-79*
- *Margaret Thatcher 1979-90*
- *John Major 1990-97*
- *Tony Blair 1997-2007*
- *Gordon Brown 2007-2010*
- *David Cameron 2010 - present*

5 ***Tony Blair was the first Prime Minister to have been born during The Queen's reign. He was born on 6th May, 1953 - a month before the Coronation.***

6 ***The Queen has attended every opening of Parliament except those in 1959 and 1963, when she was expecting Prince Andrew and Prince Edward respectively.***

7 *There have been six Archbishops of Canterbury during The Queen's reign (Archbishops Geoffrey Fisher, Michael Ramsey, Donald Coggan, Robert Runcie, George Carey and Rowan Williams).*

8 *There have been six Roman Catholic Popes during The Queen's reign (Pius XII, John XXIII, Paul VI, John Paul I, John Paul II, Benedict XVI).*

9 *The Queen has received two Popes on visits to the UK (Pope John Paul II in 1982 and Pope Benedict XVI in 2010). Pope John Paul II's visit in 1982 was the first Papal visit to the United Kingdom for over 450 years. The Queen has visited the Vatican three times in her reign – in 1961 visiting Pope John XXIII and in 1980 and 2000 visiting Pope John Paul II.*

10 *The Queen is currently Patron of over 600 charities and organisations, over 400 of which she has held since 1952.*

11 *Since 1952, The Queen has conferred over 404,500 honours and awards.*

12 *The Queen has personally held over 610 Investitures.*

13 *The first Investiture of The Queen's reign took place at Buckingham Palace on 27th February 1952. The first person to be presented was Private William Speakman, of The King's Own Scottish Borderers, who received the Victoria Cross for his actions during the Korean War.*

14 *The Queen has answered around three and a half million items of correspondence.*

15 *The Queen has sent over 175,000 telegrams to centenarians in the UK and the Commonwealth.*

16 *The Queen has sent almost 540,000 telegrams to couples in the UK and the Commonwealth celebrating their Diamond Wedding (60 years) Anniversary.*

17 *The Queen and The Duke of Edinburgh have sent approximately 45,000 Christmas cards during The Queen's reign.*

18 *The Queen has given out approximately 90,000 Christmas puddings to staff continuing the custom of King George V and King George VI.*

19 *In 60 years, The Queen has undertaken 261 official overseas visits, including 96 State Visits, to 116 different countries.*

20 *Many of The Queen's official tours were undertaken on the Royal Yacht Britannia. It was launched by Her Majesty on 16th April 1953 and was commissioned for service on 7th January 1954. It was de-commissioned in December, 1997. During this time, Britannia travelled more than a million miles on Royal and official duties.*

21 *The Royal Yacht Britannia was first used by The Queen when Her Majesty embarked with The Duke of Edinburgh on 1st May 1954 at Tobruk for the final stage of their Commonwealth Tour returning to the Pool of London. The last time The Queen was on board Britannia for an official visit was on 9th August 1997 for a visit to Arran in Scotland.*

22 *In 60 years, The Queen has often travelled to her major Realms. Her Majesty has visited Australia 16 times, Canada 22 times, Jamaica 6 times and New Zealand 10 times.*

23 *The Queen's official visits have ranged from the Cocos Islands, 5.4 square miles with a population of 596, to The Peoples' Republic of China, 3.7 million square miles with a population of 1.34 billion.*

24 *Unusual live gifts given to The Queen on foreign tours include: two tortoises given to The Queen in the Seychelles in 1972; a seven-year-old bull elephant called "Jumbo" given to Her Majesty by the President of Cameroon in 1972 to mark The Queen's Silver*

Wedding, and two black beavers given to The Queen after a Royal visit to Canada.

25 *The only time The Queen has had to interrupt an overseas tour was in 1974 during a tour of Australia and Indonesia. The Queen was called back to the UK from Australia when a general election in the UK was suddenly called. The Duke of Edinburgh continued the programme in Australia, and The Queen re-joined the tour in Indonesia.*

26 *Her Majesty's first Commonwealth tour, as Queen, began on 24th November 1953, and included visits to Canada, Bermuda, Jamaica, Panama, Fiji, Tonga, New Zealand, Australia, the Cocos Islands, Ceylon, Aden, Uganda, Libya, Malta and Gibraltar. The total distance covered was 43,618 miles.*

27 *The Queen made an historic visit to the Republic of Ireland in May 2011, the first visit by a British Monarch since Irish independence (King George V visited in 1911).*

28 *There have been 102 inward State Visits from 1952 to the end of 2011 (up to and including Turkey in November 2011).*

29 *The first football match The Queen attended was the 1953 FA Cup Final.*

30 *The Queen has laid her wreath at the Cenotaph on Remembrance Sunday every year of her reign, except in 1959, 1961, 1963, 1968, 1983 and 1999 when she was either pregnant or overseas on an official visit.*

31 *The Queen has attended 56 Royal Maundy services in 43 Cathedrals during her reign. A total of 6,710 people have received Maundy Money in recognition of their service to the Church and their communities.*

32 *The Queen has been at the saluting base of her troops in every Trooping the Colour ceremony since the start of her reign, with the exception of 1955, when a national rail strike forced the cancellation of the parade.*

33 *The Queen has attended 35 Royal Variety performances.*

34 *The Queen has launched 21 ships during her reign.*

35 *Since it was launched to mark The Queen's Golden Jubilee in 2002, The Queen's Award for Voluntary Service has been awarded to over 750 voluntary organisations across all four countries in the UK. Winners of the award have included local scout groups, community radio stations, groups who care for the elderly and environmental charities.*

36 *Over the course of the reign, almost one and a half million people have attended garden parties at Buckingham Palace or the Palace of Holyroodhouse (The Queen ended Debutante Presentation Parties in 1958).*

37 *The Queen has sat for 129 portraits during her reign.*

38 *The first 'Royal walkabout' took place during the visit by The Queen and The Duke of Edinburgh to Australia and New Zealand in 1970. The practice was introduced to allow them to meet as many people as possible, not simply officials and dignitaries.*

39 *In 1969 the first television film about the family life of the Royal Family was made, and shown on the eve of the Investiture of Prince Charles as Prince of Wales.*

40 *An important innovation during The Queen's reign was the opening in 1962 of a new gallery at Buckingham Palace to display items from the Royal Collection. The brainchild of The Duke of Edinburgh, the new Queen's Gallery occupied the space of the Palace's bomb-damaged private chapel. It was the first time that* *parts of the Palace had been opened to the general public. The new Queen's Gallery was redeveloped and re-opened in 2002 for the Golden Jubilee.*

41 *The Queen has made a Christmas Broadcast to the Commonwealth every year of her reign except 1969, when a repeat of the film 'Royal Family' was shown and a written message from The Queen issued. In 2002 The Queen made her 50th Christmas Broadcast and in 2004 The Queen made her first separate broadcast for members of the British Armed Forces.*

42 *In 1953, The Queen made the first Christmas Broadcast from overseas, (rather than from the UK), broadcasting live from New Zealand. The first televised broadcast was in 1957, made live. The first pre-recorded broadcast took place in 1960 to allow transmission around the world. In 2006 the Christmas Broadcast was first made available to download as a podcast.*

43 *The Queen launched the British Monarchy's official website in 1997. In 2007 the official British Monarchy YouTube channel was unveiled, swiftly followed by a Royal Twitter site (2009), Flickr page (2010) and Facebook page (also 2010).*

44 *The Queen hosts "theme days" and receptions to promote and celebrate aspects of British culture. Recent examples from 2011 include a reception for Young People and the Performing Arts and for Explorers. Other themes have included Publishing, Broadcasting, Tourism, Emergency Services, Maritime Day, Music, Young Achievers, British Design, and Pioneers.*

45 *In an average year, The Queen will host more than 50,000 people at banquets, lunches, dinners, receptions and Garden Parties at Buckingham Palace. The Queen also hosts more than 8,000 people each year at garden parties and Investitures at Holyroodhouse, during Holyrood Week.*

46 *The Queen was born at 17 Bruton St, London W1 on 21st April 1926, was christened on 29th May 1926 in the Private Chapel at Buckingham Palace and was confirmed on 28th March, 1942 in the Private Chapel at Windsor Castle.*

47 *The Queen learnt to drive in 1945.*

48 *With the birth of Prince Andrew in 1960, The Queen became the first reigning Sovereign to have a child since Queen Victoria, who had her youngest child, Princess Beatrice, in 1857.*

49 *The Queen's real birthday is on 21st April, but it is celebrated officially in June.*

50 *During the Silver Jubilee year, The Queen toured 36 counties in the UK and Northern Ireland, starting in Glasgow on 17th May. During her Golden Jubilee year The Queen toured 35 counties beginning in Cornwall on 1st May.*

51 *The Queen's first foreign tour of the Silver Jubilee year was a visit to Western Samoa, Tonga, Fiji, New Zealand, Australia and Papua New Guinea. The first foreign tour of The Queen's Golden Jubilee year was to Jamaica, New Zealand and Australia.*

52 *The Queen has 30 godchildren.*

53 *The Queen has owned more than 30 corgis during her reign, starting with Susan who was a present for her 18th birthday in 1944. A good proportion of these have been direct descendants from Susan. Her Majesty currently has three corgis – Monty, Willow and Holly.*

54 *The Queen also introduced a new breed of dog known as the "dorgi" when one of Her Majesty's corgis was mated with a dachshund named Pipkin which belonged to Princess Margaret. There have been 10 dorgis - Tinker, Pickles, Chipper, Piper, Harris, Brandy, Berry, Cider, Candy and Vulcan.*

The Imperial State Crown is carried out after the State Opening of Parliament.

55 *The Queen and The Duke of Edinburgh have been married for 64 years. They were married on 20th November 1947 in Westminster Abbey. The Queen's wedding dress was designed by Norman Hartnell and was woven at Winterthur Silks Limited, Dunfermline, in the Canmore factory, using silk that had come from Chinese silkworms at Lullingstone Castle.*

56 *The Queen's wedding ring was made from a nugget of Welsh gold which came from the Clogau St David's mine near Dolgellau. The official wedding cake was made by McVitie and Price Ltd, using ingredients given as a wedding gift by Australian Girl Guides.*

57 *The wedding of The Queen and The Duke of Edinburgh was the first and so far the only time in British history that the heir presumptive to the throne had been married.*

58 *The Queen's racing colours are a purple body with gold braid, scarlet sleeves and black velvet cap with gold fringe. They were adopted from those used by King Edward VII; one of his most successful horses was called Diamond Jubilee.*

59 *Queen Victoria was the last and to date the only British Monarch to celebrate a Diamond Jubilee. The Queen, who was aged 85 on Accession Day in 2012, will be the oldest Monarch to celebrate a Diamond Jubilee. Queen Victoria was 77 when she celebrated hers in 1897.*

60 *There have been only three Diamond Jubilees of Heads of State celebrated throughout the world during The Queen's reign. King Bhumibol Adulyadej of Thailand celebrated 60 years on the throne in 2006; the former Sultan of Johor (now a part of Malaysia) celebrated his in 1955; and the late Emperor Hirohito of Japan celebrated his in 1986.*

OV60 UBS